DATE DUE

NY 10 '06			

#47-0108 Peel Off Pressure Sensitive

Romancing
the Horsehide

Romancing the Horsehide

Baseball Poems on Players and the Game

by
Gene Carney

Player Silhouettes by
Mike Schacht

McFarland & Company, Inc., Publishers
Jefferson, North Carolina, and London

Acknowledgments: Mike Schacht, whose silhouettes appear among the poems collected here, has spoken more encouraging words to me than I can ever repay. He and his friends at *FAN Magazine* have offered not just moral support, but invaluable feedback. Mike's portraits suggested many of my own sketches of players.

Thanks, too, to Rick Wolff, for a shove in the right direction.

Two indispensable reference books were *The Baseball Encyclopedia* (Macmillan, 1990) and *The Ballplayers* (William Morrow, 1990), both wonderful gifts from my mother-in-law, Beverly Washburn. The small library of books in *World of Baseball* (Redefinition) was also helpful in my research of players.

Finally, thanks to my wife Barbara, for all kinds of support; and to Roger Angell, Mike Shannon, Joe Ducato, Mark Alvarez, Jack Jadick, Joe Garagiola and Bill Guilfoile.

British Library Cataloguing-in-Publication data are available

Library of Congress Cataloguing-in-Publication Data

Carney, Gene, 1946–
    Romancing the horsehide : baseball poems on players and the game / by Gene Carney.
        p.   cm.
    ISBN 0-89950-838-3 (lib. bdg. : 55# alk. paper) ∞
    1. Baseball players—Poetry.   2. Baseball—Poetry.   I. Title.
PS3553.A755R65   1993
811'.54—dc20   92-42356
                                                                          CIP

Manufactured in the United States of America

McFarland & Company, Inc., Publishers
  Box 611, Jefferson, North Carolina 28640

Table of Contents

Foreword

I wrote my first baseball poem when I was ten or eleven, and it wasn't for school. I was newly smitten with the sport, and my poem's title shows that: "The World's Greatest Game." As I recall, it was, like "Casey," long and rhyming, and described a single game set somewhere outside of time. I left my readers hanging at the end, with the game on the line, bases loaded, two down, full count, and so on. Casey fanned and took all joy from Mudville; I wanted my readers to have joy forever, to enjoy the suspense, no matter which side they took.

I wish the same for readers of this book. I hope ten-year-olds read it and then go on to read the wonderful biographies and other books that are available today. I hope their parents find themselves taken not so much back into time as out of it, into the special world that is baseball.

A Baseball Family Album

Without the iconic numbers
Like Cy's 511, Ted's .406, the Babe's 60
Without the fabulous legends
Tall tales of Josh's homers that land
In the next city on the next day
Without the headlines and box scores
They are still there

We recognize their faces
From black-and-white photos
And newsreels and pieces
Of cardboard that sold tobacco
Their trademark stances
Windups and deliveries
Slings and swings
Trots around the sacks
Head-first slides home

They have become family
Sometimes we know their nicknames
Best of all
No one is anonymous
And each has left something behind
Not just the tools of their craft
Horsehide and leather
White ash and muddy metal cleats
Pinstriped jerseys and wire-rimmed sunglasses
Not just trophies and rings and the stuff
Of attic trunks and gameroom displays

We have memories
Stories told between generations
Embellished over hot stoves
Recalled every summer
In the grandstand and bleachers
When something out there jogs
Something in here
Where they will live
As long as the Game
Is played

Resin Bag's Complaint

Don't mind that the jerk
Spikes me into the mound
After his gophers—
Used to getting kicked around
After ball four
Or the two-bagger
Or the easy out thrown away
By the rookie at short

What gripes me
Is that after krucial Ks
When *I* make the decisive difference
In the special spin and determining direction
Not to mention the pivotal placement
And significant speed
When *I* leave the swinger
Blowin' in the wind
He takes all the credit
As if *his* sweaty digits
Might have managed it by themselves
Without my amazing saving grace

Do you want to know a secret?
(Long as I have your ear)
Just once
I'd like to take that trip home
Like the hard guy with the seams
And the fancy autograph on his backside

Let me dodge the lumber
Or kill *my*self trying
Let *me* have the dignity of risk
That you grant daily
Those mud-dulled
Multi-stitched
Hide-bound windings
Of yarn over
Rubber over
Cork

Dutch Master

Five June days
In his twenty-third summer
Guaranteed his name
A permanent niche
In the sport's memory
Johnny Double No-Hit
Vander Meer

No-no's are stewed
In pressure cookers
The late-inning tension
Growing more terrible by the pitch
Isolating the hurler
Silencing his dugout
Causing the noise in the stands
To pulsate in exaggerated whoops
For each fresh out
Then each strike
Finally to burst
With relief
The collective pain
Of birthing
Over

Just once so far
Has the game borne twins

Under Ebbets' vogue lights
Johnny on the spot
This time from the get-go
Prepared from his first high hard one
To tip his hat and celebrate again
His notable nine
When the end inevitably arrived

Instead
Here we go again
Flirting time

Double the tension
Triple the collective pain
But multiply by forty thousand
Cheering in the waiting room
The joy of delivery
Cigars all around
For the Dutch Master

Johnny Vander Meer

3

Shoeless Joe

How he loved her
How he used her

She was never heavy to him
But the perfect fit
What a pair they were
Summer after summer:
Joe and Betsy

He called her black and beautiful
She responded to his touch
By springing to life
Charm for no one but Joe

Traveled with him from Philly
To Cleveland to Chicago
Betsy brought him luck
Until that terrible day
They were split up
By the Mountain Man

Cut down in his prime
Accusations hurled by gamblers
Jackson said it wasn't so
Betsy protested loudly
But the hanging judge had spoken
The fatal word

Torn from his trademark and trade
Banished to roam the countryside
Aching with all his soul
For a reunion that would never happen

How he loved her
How he used her
She was everything to him
Betsy was never just
Joe's bat

Joe Jackson

4

Field of Dreams

Yeah, guess I'm a member of AA:
Alienated by Astroturf
Hey, most of us never played on plastic
Grass is the missing link
Between all the games of our lives—
Sandlot, Little League, school—
And theirs

But why stop at replanting the real green?
Why not make the playing fields
Even more connecting?

Let's plant trees around the outfield
Let the warning track burst into colors
For the Series

Let the outfielders fish around in thorny bramble
For lost balls in the gaps
(Both sides hunt till it's found)

Let the thieves slide into flat rocks
That don't give anything but bruises

Let glass windows be
Strategically placed
Near the bullpens, maybe
Batters breaking them get the bases
But it costs them ten thou each
(The fines go to charity)

Let the field of our dreams
Have its cornfield in right center
Ground rule double in the stalks
Let vendors sell the cobs: "Souven-*ears*, here!"

Let the infield undulate some
With a sprinkling of pebbles
To keep those wizards on their toes

Let all fielders wear gloves
Without all that trapping and padding
So their hands sting some—
The price of earned POs and A's

Let them keep the ball in play
As in the days before the Babe
Til they knock the covers off
Keep tape handy for extra innings
Now there's a game worth the price of admission.

Mickey

No mining lead and zinc for Mutt's boy
Gave him a ballplayer's name
Taught him to hit from both sides
Before he could bicycle
Taught him the way out
Taught him The Game

Mickey's lightning legs took him
The rest of the way
Up the alphabet
Beyond Triple-A
To the Stadium

Look up tape-measure home run
Three-point-one to first on the drag bunt
That's Mutt Mantle's kid

Look up World Series
Hall of Fame
That's Mutt's Triple-Crown Mickey

In the sport's geneology
He descends directly from DiMaggio
But the kid from Oklahoma
Will always be
Mutt's pride of the Yankees
And joy of his heart

Mickey Mantle

Tape Measure

Not everyone could hit
Tape-measure home runs
Mickey could:
Pinstriped slashes echoing the Babe's
Dotted lines in the photo next day
Tracing the imaginary flight into history

As a kid
I often wondered where they got
That five-hundred-plus-foot ribbon
Hauled out to the stadiums
From the nearest university
I guessed
By a crack team of
Bespeckled bearded scientists
In white lab coats
Carrying clipboards and rulers
And Lord knows what else they used
To make their measurements

Today I realize
They were probably just guys
Looking for free passes

Science in those days
Was as welcome in the game
As it was in religion:
Not much at all

Who cared *exactly* how far it went?
The more important questions were
Was it done in the clutch?
And did it win a game?
And whose did it remind you of?
If the smash set off a chain reaction
Of storytelling for the next week
Then it was
Long enough

The Flying Dutchman

Is there a greater irony
Than that Sweet Caporal tobacco card
Selling in today's marketplace
For more than twice the Dutchman ever earned
In his radiant score of seasons?

Its unimaginable value the result
Of Honus' contempt
For opportunistic bucks

Hans alone just said No
To those who would buy his soul
Disdain
As rare then as now

Triple threat
He manufactured victories
With his tools of wood and leather
His bowlegged base-to-base swiftness
And play
Hard as the spikes
That carried him home

How fitting it is the face of Wagner—
The Pirate who loved the game so much
That he'd have suited up for nothing—
Even on that cardboard scrap
He gazes with clear conscience
His life and livelihood uncompromised
A snapshot from the less-traveled road

Honus Wagner

Baseball Cards

Our sons shake their heads
They don't understand
How we could have lost
Those Mantle rookies
Early Aarons
And sophomore Stargells
Not just a single star
But whole galaxies
Swallowed up in black holes
Long gone

Of course if our generation
Had hung on
Those cardboard rectangles
Would not be worth all that much today
To our collecting sons
Would they?
Can't have it both ways

Worth
Is in the eye of the kid
Beholding a likeness he sees
In his favorite team's colors
At the ballpark or on TV—
Paper companion to
An autographed plastic & foam seat cushion
Or a newspaper clipping from that day
He became the batting champ
Of one lad's heart

Even as we stuck the cards in bike wheels
Or flipped and pitched them
Snapping them fiercely against concrete
Even then some were special

Would we sell them today?
What would it profit us
To gain transitory bucks
But lose reminders
Of the way we were?

That much?
Well, that's different

Yet no one can purchase memories
Connections with first heroes
Access to the seasons of our
Infatuation

Jackie

When his name comes up
We always see Robinson in our mind's eye
Dancing off third

His own eyes fixed on the windup
He's ready to go
Electricity
Poised to shock and thrill
Dust never settling near his cleats
He's wired to break
Steal a run or a game
To win

Of course
It's the riskiest move in the game
But he was used to dares
Hero or goat
Once he said Yes to Mr. Rickey
He was destined to be one or the other
Stealing home must have seemed
Child's play
To Jackie
A chance to move on
Instead of just enduring

First black man in the Promised Land
Modern Moses delivering in the clutch
His rookie season screamed
To the pharoahs of the game:
Let my people play

Barreling down the line
Parting seas of bigotry
His dash home
Could no longer be blocked
His dark finger on the white
Spelling victory
For everyone

Jackie Robinson

The Mahatma

Mr. Rickey's nickname
Suggests a wise man
With a great soul
And prestige
Yet it sounds foreign

And perhaps he was
From a different world
From the future

A world where the Game
Thrived on talent
Mined by sharp eyes
And then raised on farms
To be harvested for
The tops of the pyramids

A world where the Game
Demanded spring rehearsals
Where mechanical arms
Tossed tirelessly to helmeted men
Inside cages

A world where the Game
Was played color-blind
No Jackie needed
To make the teams reflect
The human rainbow
Of their cities and towns

Shrewd bow-tied lawyer
Branch Rickey
Puffed about the Game
Clouds of cigar smoke
And when they cleared
The Game had changed
Its very soul becoming
A little greater

Bambino

Season by season
Swat by swat
Without TV
With only newsreel movies
And press headlines
The Babe escaped boxscore
Sports section
Sport
And grew into folk hero

Conformity was a pitch he sent sailing
Ruth was as hard to manage by pitchers
(Or batters, when he was on the hill)
As by coaches and teammates
Everyday life became a mix
Of legend and events
Called shots and cured tots
Swirling among those Ruthian numbers

More popular than presidents
The Babe was permitted
And forgiven all
For being wealthy when most were poor
Brash when most were meek
For being a rebel without a cause
Except the old ball game

Ruth confirmed with his crowns and titles
That America needed no royalty
But his own
Anyone could make superstar
If that ugly saloon-keeper's kid
Who winked like a con man
Could wash the sport's black sox clean

Season by season
Swat by swat
He grew in our imagination and
Childlike eyes
By being himself
Standing against that profound current
Babe Ruth   Which would make us all less

Damn Yankees

(A Review)

How wonderful that this musical ends
With the Senators on top
Joe Hardy's team destined
To defeat the damn New Yorkers
Over and over and forever
A rare enough event
When they played the game in D.C.

Today the deal struck with Applegate
Would begin with the return of the franchise
And end with Joe being
The last of the free agents
Fought over by a dozen teams
("Whatever Lola Wants" reworked)
In the mother of all bidding wars

The notion of anyone wanting just a pennant
Too incredible
For today's sophisticated audiences
The notion of loyalty
Too far-fetched
The stuff of fiction and nostalgia
To understand either notion
You gotta have heart

Yankee Clipper

Joe D. was born in 1914
Same as my Dad
Who's long gone now

Joe's still with us
Although that song keeps asking
Where he's gone
As if he has
As if we'd ever let him
Be lost to memory

Joe D. played center stage
Center city
When baseball was center sport
There his style and class
Refracted the limelight
Like a perfectly cut diamond

The Streak
Was like that final burst
Of color and illumination
At the finish
Of a 4th of July fireworks show
Perfect for timeless association
With Mr. Consistency

Joe D. was born on November 25
Same as my Little Leaguer son
Any father would be proud
To see DiMaggio's thing reflected
Even a little
In his offspring
Not the numbers
But the consistent effort
Poise in the noise
Uncommon grace
Presence
Old-fashioned pride
In his work

Joe DiMaggio

14

Streaks

No common baseball phenomenon
Is so unpredictable
As a streak

The game is such a slave
To the law of averages
That the temporary releases
Cause euphoria (if winning)
Or clinical depression (if losing)

Every contest is a coin flip
And though we know each day
Is its own
We remember that we came up
Heads
Yesterday
And the day before
And how long can this go on?

In the euphoria and depression
(Heads or tails)
Is something eerie and
Other-worldly
The end of a streak
Thus brings relief
For a return to the world
Where it's comfortably
Average
Again and again

So we marvel to learn
Of McGraw's 1916 Giants
Who won 17 on the road early on
And 26 at home toward the end
But finished
Fourth

Streaks are exhilarating
As rollercoaster rides
Terrifying and tear-making
White-knuckle times
Yet the races are won
By teams that stride down the
  midway
Without being distracted by the
  amusements
Save their coins for the stretch
And enjoy most of all
The reward earned by
Hard work
Over the long haul

Double X

Jimmie slugged X-rated homers
Renowned more for their violent sound
Than for their prodigal trajectory

Protégé of H. R. Baker
Schooled in Connie Mack's dugout
Until he burst forth
With a dozen summers
Of thirty-plus power
Beastly biceps on display
And delivering

Intimidating from the on-deck circle
Foxx amplified the force
Of those fortunate to bat ahead
Simmons at Shibe
Or Ted in the Monster's shadow
Enemy pitchers saw the approach
Of Jimmie's broad shoulders
Imagined his long strides
And pondered the containment
Of the impending blast

The extra X marked the spot
In Chicago and Cleveland and New York
And almost every AL park
Where the tape-measure stopped
And the tales started

Include this gentle giant
With Gehrig and Greenberg and Mize
In any hot stove debate about
Who's on First
Forever

Jimmie Foxx

Bucketfoot Al

Simmons roared in with the Twenties
Solid as Shibe's concrete and steel
He became a royal member
Of Mack's second dynasty
Forming with Foxx and Cochrane
A terrorist trio of Killer A's

Al's bucketfoot stance
Drew skeptical chuckles
Only until the game was afoot
As his long bat lashed out
Sprays of long liners
The flaw became a warning:
This pale Pole showed no mercy
In the war he declared
On all hurlers

Snapshots of this warrior
Are all slightly blurred:
His snare of the long fly
That tried to be Gehrig's
Fifth homer that game —
Crucial late-inning clouts
(Sleeves flapping on the slides)
Or October thunder —
Even his notable K
In Hubbell's starry string
Reminds us of how this man
Hit

Al Simmons

17

Irreconcilable Differences

Divorce
Is roughest on the kids.
They've grown accustomed to his face
On their T-shirts
And the posters in their bedrooms.
They know his stance
His Topps card
They have his autograph
On a scorecard.

Their dads say they understand
He took the best deal
Loyalty's for royalty
And all that.

But the kids only know
That he's gone
And has left behind a void
That will never be completely filled.
Ever.

Free agency isn't free.
It costs tears
That taste
Like the end of childhood.

Ralph

Hero without a nickname
When New York had its Clipper
Boston its Splendid Kid
And St. Louis its Man
Star without a galaxy
Pittsburgh's Ralph

Heir to Greenberg's Gardens and his wisdom
Kiner lit up and filled up Forbes
His first seven summers in the show
Topping the league in homers each season
Twice over the nifty fifty mark
Without a supporting cast
Ralph stole the show

Suddenly he was gone
"Traded"—as if anyone
Could equal his worth
For those who clicked the turnstiles
Just for Ralph
Left behind were the echoes
Of Ruthian cracks
(With Ruthian frequency)
Aunt Minnie's broken windows
Adoring unending
Cheers

The sounds were long gone
Like a trademark hit
No joy in Iron City:
Pirate treasure overboard

Ralph Kiner

Rainout

The tarp
Is the saddest of sights

How we booed
When it was rolled out
Even though we knew
It was inevitable

How we'll cheer
When and if
It is finally
Dragged into the outfield
And relieved of its burden
The stuff puddles are made of

The tarp
Has turned us all
Into clock-watchers

We came to escape time
And now we can only
Endure

Stubs

What is it
About ticket stubs
That prevents me
From throwing them away

Not just the precious few
From a World Series
But lately
I can't throw *any* away

They do not bring to mind
Vivid memories
Of good times
Or remembrances
Of hits and runs past

Yet they stand for something
For times I traveled
Outside of time
Like stamped passports
They are all the proof remaining
Of my trips

Iron Horse

What's in a nickname?
Lou's was
A tale of two eras

The horse was power
Before planes trains and automobiles
Natural brawny native
Tame to the eye but always wild
Galloping past broken-down buggies
To spaces where no tracks had been laid

Iron had its virtues
Durable hard strong
Locomotive stuff
Crossing the land without rest
Putting towns and cities on the map

The Iron Horse took the field
Season after shining season
Enduring as no one before or since

His accomplishments in the game
Hardly suggest a career
Cut short
His final seasons spent courageously
Slugging against an invisible hurler
A disease destined to strike out
"The luckiest man on the face of the earth"

Iron rusts and horses die
We know all that
Yet Gehrig's words jar and haunt us
Our nickname
Was supposed to
Let him play
Forever

Lou Gehrig

The Old Arbitrator

Klem was the rock
Upon which was built
Respect
For the law
And the order
Umps enforce
To make possible
Play

To be labeled "Fair":
Is there a greater compliment
To seek
In any profession?

The lines he drew
In the dust of diamonds
No doubt infuriated those who knew
The step across
Put them in the showers

The lines set boundaries
As Bill's manner
Set patterns
For generations
Of men in black

"Never missed one"
Proclaimed the authority
"In my heart"
Added the man

Besides the calls of
Fair or foul
Strike or ball
Bill Klem
Took his games
Safely out of dispute
And made the fields
Even

The Umpire

Calls 'em as he sees
Calls 'em quick and right
Always right
'Cause what he calls and sees
Goes

His best performances
Are as unremarkable
As the rubber slab on the mound
Part of the setting
Blends in
Hidden
Fans go home bubbling about
Wow catches or the amazing grace
Of the shortstop with in-line cleats
About hits or misses in the clutch
Or the way the home team's pen
Was mightier than the visitors' swords

Only TV watchers
Privy to replays
Can have frame-by-frame appreciation
Can ooh and aah
The super call in the collision at third

At the park
The umpire is
The lightning rod for wrath
Never to be cheered
High priest of the ritual
Conductor of magic to the people
Their return of praise
Soars on by past him
To the Game

Little Napoleon

John McGraw
Fundamentalist before the
Fundamentals got around
Baseball's answer to Franklin and Edison
Old Oriole invented new ways to win
Every time his team took the field

So much of baseball's family
Bears a strong resemblance
To this patriarch of the inside game
His genes dominant as his Giants
In the scrappy skippers who fight
Tooth and nail for their players
And their victories
Anything goes
For the generals at war

The game has his eyes
Nothing escaped them
No opportunity
For the extra base or run
No chance to cut down the enemy rally
Or slow the enemy runner
No occasion to instruct
Motivate
Lead

Eyes lit by fire
Eyes for talent buried in
Sons of miners and farmers
Eyes for intimidating
Authorities upstairs or between the lines
And all those not on his side
Eyes for the advantage everywhere
His armies hit and ran
Like Colonial soldiers
Disciplined by a tyrant
Tactics was Mr. McGraw's
Business

John McGraw

24

The Manager

Chessmaster
Calculator
Gambler

From the posting of the lineup
To the toasting of the win
Or the roasting in the postgame
Sound bites and columnist backbites
He is where the game unfolds

His infield will creep in to strangle
Enemy runners invading home space
Or back off for the sure one
To play it safe
Or press, force, steal the base
The advantage
The infinitely precious W

He alone may yank
Due batter for the pinch
Waning flamer for the fireman
Free-swinger for the gentle bunter
Leaky glove for genuine leather

He alone has pitchers pause
To purposefully pass or
To go after his
Assuming the other general
Lets his soldier
Stand and try to deliver

Now he is the Thinker
His strategy bubbles to the surface
In tandem with those in the nearby cooler
Now he is the Doer
Charging from his safe haven
A lion from a dugout den
To challenge the masked man in blue
To give voice to what twenty-five
Or twenty-five thousand
Feel in their hearts
Sherlock's famous logic doomed
In this and every novel
To be overthrown by Moriarty's calls

The Old Professor

Casey learned the game
From the ancient Orioles
McGraw and Robinson
Learned how to get
From here to October
And what to do
When the world is a Series
And lightning is needed
To bring home the ring

Casey played the game
Like a daffy Dodger
Ex- and inciting fans
Charming and disarming umps
Clown with some clout
Stengel had a major-league eye
And knew when to wink

Casey taught the game
To the new Yankees
Mickey and Whitey and Gil and Yogi
To his kids
Taught them not to settle for
Seasons that ended in September
Taught in his own language
Those who would listen and decipher
Learned to win

You could look up
Casey Stengel
Through all of the pages
Between the fading of the dead ball
And the arrival of the Amazin' Mets
Casey's purgatory
After the bliss of his Bronx dynasty
You could look him up:
Just watch for the jester
Wearing the crown and the grin

Pennant Race

At the start of the marathon
Everybody's even
And it looks like
Each team has a chance
To finish first

By the first turn of months
A few are already
Dropping back
Too far to recover

At the All-Star break
Rotations can be set again
But there's not much real rest
For the contenders
Not much of a break, really
The standings stand pat
No jockeying for position
Not even a chance to gain
A half-game

Most teams wilt in the heat
Of July and August
As the pace needed to win
Is finally known

Labor Day is the signal
For the final laps
Around the league
Time to sprint for those who can
Time to hope for miracles
Pressure-cooker time
Even as life goes back to school

By October everyone knows
That the games won
Were less important
Than the series lost
And that the series won
Were less important
Than the weeks lost
And that the weeks of streaks
When winning came easy
Count less in the end
Than hard months of productive toil
One game, one inning
One out at a time

The Lip

Leo was not a nice guy
No matter where he finished
In his half century with the Game

His glove was mightier than his bat
Captain of the Gashouse
Never just one of the Gang
That might have been his epitaph
But he lived on

Skipper in Flatbush
He was Ensign Pulver cast as Queeg
And finally as Ahab
Destined to help Jackie aboard
And shatter the Great White
That might have been his epitaph
But he lived on

When he made the short jump of ships
He found himself at the helm
For Thomson's round-the-world cruise
And for the arrival of a real Giant:
Willie was destined to bring fame
To whomever penciled in his name
That might have been Durocher's epitaph
But he lived on

On into his fifties and sixties
Into the sixties and seventies
Leo penciled in nearly four thousand lineups
Might have been around at the end of more games
But for his amplifying Lip
And because he lived on and on
We have our choice of words
For this man of choice words
For Leo Durocher's epitaph

Coach

The crack of the bat
Starts inside your head
A cascade of calculations

How deep the hit
To how deep a glove
And opposite that gloved hand
How strong and straight the arm
That would nail if it could
Your charge tagging on third
(How sturdy *his* legs)
Burden too precious to waste
On whimsy

As the fly peaks
Starts its dwindling dive
Focused fielder taps his
Fine leathered friend
Inching backward and
Getting ready to charge plateward
To make his seize while on the tear
Shifting his momentum to the orb
To gain the edge of a second's fraction
Your runner braces
Sprinter on starting blocks
Straining for your pistol shot
"GO!"

Now you blend with the stadium crowd
Your job done
You are a spectator
Enjoy the race between man and agate
To the human goes the credit
Should he win
If the agate
To you the blame
Unknown hero or public bum
A wonderful life
For the cool judge
Near the hot corner

Doubleheader

An unspoiled beach
We could drive there like sixty with no jams
To sip from nickel coke bottles
And read dime magazines
For a quarter of a day

Past pleasures no lottery windfall
Can ever quite buy back
Any more than our innocence then
In those days of
Sunday Doubleheaders

With Mom's lunch to eat between games
We arrived early and began praying Sweep
And stayed till the scoreboard sagged
From the weight of thirty-two hung panels
Announcing the outcomes of the day's battles
On our field and around the leagues

In the grandstand shade
We hoarsened ourselves
Spilling peanut shells as we stood for the long hits
Stinging our hands in claps for hometown K's
Scorecard pencils nubs needing relief
Like a spent starter

Opener dropped
Consolation found in a nightcap triumph
Bitterness in a second defeat
But what can compare
To the bliss of Two in One
The W column swells today
As grand as the tide
Over an unspoiled beach

Smoky Joe

The nickname was a perfect fit
Steam comparable to the Big Train
His summer dueling partner

The dream season of 1912
Hints at his stuff
Thirty-eight times he took the hill
Thirty-five times he was there at the end
Ten times unscored upon
Thirty-five victories in hand
Probably talked more about his
Fifteen extra-base hits
And .290 average

When a thumb injury
Finally forced him off the mound
Wood took some time off
Then declared himself
A ballplayer

The smoke changed directions
Now it was his bat on fire
For five more summers

Like only a handful of others
Including the Babe
Smoky Joe Wood might have made the Hall
For his deeds on the rubber
Or in the batter's box
Had he been inducted he probably
Would have talked more about his son
Pitcher for the Red Sox

Joe Wood

Spahnie

The older this dog became
The more tricks he added

Overhand destroyer of timing
Spahn made winning twenty
A habit
And a trademark

Veteran before rookie
As hard to root against
As he was to defeat

My own book on Spahnie
As a Pirate fan
Said to get to him early
Or wait till tomorrow

I looked forward in those days
To the All-Star games and the Series
When I could root for the NL ace
With a clear conscience

While he was climbing that hill toward 300
We kept thinking back to those empty years
Wondering if his over-seasons
Spent in the uniform of his Uncle
Would keep him from reaching the top

When he hit the peak
Without breaking stride
And kept climbing
We realized bravery in action
Was this guy's thing

After the Purple Heart
The Cy Young took on a perspective
His Cooperstown plaque
A more facile bronze than his
Star

Warren Spahn

Eyewitness Account

Spahnie's first pitch
Was delivered with the expected
Yet stunning suddenness
Of the opening four notes
Of a famous Fifth Symphony
Sinking low and away
On the final note
In harmony with the thud
Into Crandall's target
And Jocko's "Steee-rike!"

Thus the conductor took the lead
Knitting together that strand
With three more darters
To form a perfect leadoff K

Hitters who failed to remember
How they went down the last time
Were condemned to repeat

In the seventh
Spahnie started the coda:
The late innings were *his*
There were nine Braves out there
But no one could take their eyes off
This professional working man

Warren Spahn was simply
The best I ever saw at his craft
Pitching to win
And even though I had to root against him
Something in me always rooted for him
He earned my respect and admiration
Without saying a word

Horsehide

In my neighborhood
Baseballs
Went through stages:

New balls were
Too beautiful to be used

Finally scuffed
And grass-stained
They entered the arena
For bloody combat
To the death

Who knows how many times
We clubbed it
Before it shed its skin
Stiff and in form
Like a snake's

Someone ran home for tape
And soon it was back in action
Black and shiny
If the tape was electrical
Of if adhesive
Mummified in royal white
A toy for a Pharaoh's son

Big Train

If there are zeroes on the scoreboard
And smoke between the mound and the batter's box
Walter's probably out there tossing
His speed

Pity the poor backstop
His hands punished by the thuds
Velocity that radar guns
Could only dream about tracking

While his Senators filibustered runs
The Big Train smashed home
Clearing batsmen off the rails
Pounding like ocean waves on boulders
As awesome a sight as a coastal storm
A feast of wind and sound

The Big Train smashed home
Carving over the years a grand canyon
Making forever marks on the face of the game
Five score and ten shutouts
A pile of W's 416 high
And an upper-deck row of K's
That stretch from the Capitol to Cooperstown
Johnson was the other
Washington Monument

Walter Johnson

Three-Finger

The seventh summer
Of any boy's life
Can be an awakening of sorts
Join the gang
Try your hand at new sports
For Mordecai Peter Centennial Brown
It was clearly a turning point
Thanks to his uncle's corn-cutter:
Took his fingers
Gave him an arsenal

Ace of the Cubbie dynasty
He hurled like he wanted
To stay out of the coal mines
The job he had before this one

Take a time-machine ride back
To see the craftsman Brown at work
Chances are
Matty's on the hill for the Giants
Three-Finger and Christy
Batters beware
Sure better play for one run today
Goose eggs in the air
Sudden death from the first pitch
Mordecai hurled like he knew the cost
Of one mistake
In any inning of life

Mordecai Brown

First Ball

Presidents do it
Celebrities do it
Once even all the fans did it
(Thanks to Veeck—who else?)
Let's do it
Let's fall in—
Wait a minute here

Is there a ceremony less useful
Than the lame toss of the
First spring albino robin's egg?
Half the time the play is muffed
The ball is never put in the game anyway
And a few innings later
Half the crowd would flunk a pop quiz
On who threw

I propose that if the ritual persists
As most do
Then let the virgin sphere be cast
By no one older than ten
If they can define free agency
They're disqualified
And no famous kid movie stars either

Let American springs burst forth
With wide-eyed tykes
Bubble-gum in cheek
Uniformed or pure sandlot
Freckled and wrinkled and
Agog with the wonder of their years

Let them be annual reminders—
Give the formality a new meaning
Let their eyes teach us all
Even the prodigal sons of guns
The word we almost said before
Love
Of the Game

Chief

Charley Bender was no Sockalexis
Cleveland's original Indian
And a hard act to follow
But he was proud
Of his Chippewa heritage
Without reservation

Before he was twenty
He was in the A's rotation
With Plank and Waddell
Then in the first Mack Dynasty
Became a Series regular

Bender drew plenty of praise
(Cobb: "brainiest" pitcher faced)
But forget the words
He pitched the must-win games
The ones on the way to pennants
Or up against Mathewson
Duels in the cool October sun

He was no Chief, of course
But on the mound
Clearly he was in charge
Hostilities toward his race
Reduced to the one-on-one
Between himself and the batter
Bender fit only the stereotype
Of the clutch winner

Satchel

The very names of his teams
Stir up other-worldly visions·
Birmingham Black Barons
Nashville Elite Giants
Chattanooga Black Lookouts
Crawfords and Monarchs
Stars and the Black Sox
They weren't turned out
But never let in either

The very names of his pitches
Stir up colorful visions:
Little Tom and Long
Radio and B Balls
Two-hump blooper
And the hesi-
Tation

In a game where records
Are part of the mystique
Satchel's birth date was uncertain
Seemed like he was born pitching
And destined to throw forever
Always with style
His own

Even then
In his four decades
Mostly in the shadows
Before the awful eclipse ended
There was no one like
Lanky Leroy Paige
Don't bother to look back

Did that oldest rookie ever die
Or does he live on yet
Folk hero separate but equal
Always somewhat separate
Always at least equal

Satchel Paige

39

Ol' Stubblebeard

Burleigh was surly
His spitters no crimes
The last of the legals
Ol' Stubblebeard Grimes

He had the demeanor
Of Billy Goat Gruff
His pitches were weighted
With plenty of stuff

Intimidation
Was his middle name
Bullied his pass
To the game's Hall of Fame

Burleigh saw baseball
As kaleidoscope matter
Subtle in patterns
But no use for the batter

Durable thrower
He mixed in choice curves
Batting up against Grimes
Was a battle of nerves

We can only guess how
He'd have played his career
With one fewer pitch
To stick in your ear

Burleigh Grimes

Hoot

For most of the sixties
And a few years after
Bob Gibson was
The Cardinal rule

This terrorist was known
Not just for where
He tossed his exploding grenades
(The inside of the plate was his—
Let the crowder beware)
But how:
An old-fashioned arm pump
Then a trademark whirl that
Lifted him
And us

In between heaves
Gibby was all eyes:
They seemed to burn past batters
And focus on the padded backstop
Who was shielded from the glare
And who dared not disturb
The rhythm of the executions

The cool of October's games
Only revved up his heat a notch:
Seven W's in nine tries
Punctuated by scores of clutch K's—
Gibson was at home
Taking the hill for
Game seven

Bob Gibson

41

Dizzy

Shooting star
He flashed so loudly and brightly
In his abbreviated time before us
That the impression was lasting

He may indeed have been the greatest
As he said
For that time
Cockiness enough to fill a Gashouse
His fireballs backing up his brags
And making his predictions come true

The X-rays lied:
Plenty in Dean's bean, all right
Some of it slud out later over the radio
A lot of it got packaged
But the bulk was focused
On Cardinal foes digging in
Turning ABs into Ks

His last game is a clue to the character:
Challenged out of retirement
Out from behind his famous mike
A decade after his All-Star toe
Dampened his glowing arm
He started tossing goose eggs all over again
Just for show
Just for *the* show
Til his hamstringed body
Made him quit all over again

Never a case of mind over matter
For Diz
But a matter of minding
How the matter was encased
If he said something was gold
It was damn well going to glitter

Sandy

Crowd into the stadium
On the day Koufax is throwing
And enjoy the anticipation

Keep your eye on the ball
While he lobs his first warmups
Pretty soon it will be just a blur
Something in the vicinity of
The opposition swings
Rumored to be solid

Get set to fill your scorecard
With K's—some twisted around
Like the fanning batters
Start counting—
Double-digits in whiffs today?

Probably not too many runs on deck
The Dodgers will scratch for their few
Maybe one will be enough—
After all, Sandy's on the mound

If he's *really* on
Then watch out—
Anything can happen
How long since his *last* no-no?
What would today's make it?

Sandy's career was
Six years of wrestling for control
And a half dozen of being there
Being on top of his profession
Glowing in the Octobers
He earned for his team
A nova increasingly brilliant
Then suddenly gone

Sandy was still just thirty
So much was ahead
How many more shutouts
Southpaw strikeouts
And low-hit gems?
Come to the stadium still
Scan the leagues
For fire-ballers who dream of being
The next Koufax

Sandy Koufax

Cy

How ya gonna keep the boy from Ohio
Down on the farm
With an arm like *that*?

Cleveland's Spiderman
Lightning spinnings tied up his prey
Mismatched
Their sticks
Against his fog

Colossus of country roads
Winning ballgames was as ordinary for Cy
As doing the chores
Pitching hay or nickel curves
Breaking bats or topsoil
Warming up wastes sunlight
Do what you're there to do
Pursue the outs one at a time
Excellence found in the unhurried pace
No need to think about it much
Once it's become routine

Maybe in his case
A single number *is* a fair description:
511
When it came to winning
Nobody did it better
Won twenty in his off-seasons
Thirty or more, five times
But never got the Award
Didn't need any blue ribbons
Save them for the livestock at the fair
Denton True *was*
Cy Young

Cy Young

Lefty

Four decades before Carlton
Five years before Gomez
Appeared the southpaw
Known ever since as Lefty

Work in the coal mines
Fueled his catapult blazers;
Blowing glass taught him
The fine artistry of curves
And the symmetry
Reflected some in his
Precisely three hundred wins
And an equal number of games finished

Grove in the groove:
Backbone of the rotation and
Awesome as the dynastic A's offense
In those three splendid seasons
Philly escaped depression—
When they ruled the AL
Murdering the Bronx row—
Lefty's 31 in '31
(Following 28 in the Year of the Hitter)
The perfect harmonious climax
For patriarch Cornelius' crew

Cochrane's one finger down
Meant ornery fast balls
White grapes of wrath
From the terrible swift hurler
With the matching disposition
Lefty and losing didn't mix:
Stand back when they
Shared the same locker

Fellers like Koufax
Nolan and Roger the Rocket
Stir in our memories
The smooth warm light of
Robert Moses Grove's
Fiery left arm

The Whip

Six-six beanpole
Remembered most for
The way he threw
Ewell Blackwell
His name was within two outs
Of being linked forever
With Vander Meer

Wicked
Nasty
Vicious
These were some of the printables
Right-handed batters used
To describe his sidearm slings

Swooshing in a white blur
From third base
Freezing
Intimidating
Backing off
When the whip cracked
Hitters listened

We saw only glimpses
Of what might have been
Had the whip not given out early:
Streak of sixteen wins
Topping the league in
Shutouts as a rookie
Strikeouts and wins
That second summer
When he just missed
The no-no-no-no

Ewell Blackwell

No matter—
From then on
Whenever Blackwell
Took the hill for Cincinnati
The air hummed with possibilities
The way it's supposed to
In baseball

Rapid Robert

On his Iowa farm
His father planted a home plate
And a pitching rubber
Seeds that produced
A Cooperstown arm

Young Bob threw every day
Winters in the barn
Helped build a real Field for Dreams
Grandstand behind first
Scoreboard for the zeroes
And finally he came

Cy was no Shoeless Joe
Scout offered only a buck
And a baseball full of names
With room for one more
Bob's ticket East

Cleveland's Rapid Transit
To runs at October
Official scorers' panacea
Just stamp the book with K's

His missing seasons
Were spent throwing in loyal Navy blue
Not just entertaining his uncle's kids
But hurling against enemy strikers in the Pacific
In an opposite reality

When Feller's heat was turned up
Safeties became endangered
In three games extinct
In a dozen others reduced to one

Was it velocity
That made this Indian a winner:
Veering white
Mixed up with dead man curves?
Or was it something else from the farm
Grown up inside the boy
Good stuff
Of manhood

Bob Feller

47

Harvey on the Mound

The outlook wasn't brilliant
    for the Pittsburgh nine that night.
They'd played twelve scoreless with the Braves
    and still no end in sight.
Their pitcher had been perfect,
    setting down all thirty-six
But now was brewing trouble
    and it looked grim for Haddix.

The lead-off Brave got on, you see,
    on the defense's only blunder.
A bunt moved up that tainted man
    and brought up Aaron's thunder.
But Hank was passed, of course,
    to let him swing—pure folly
So to the plate strode Joe Adcock
    A tough out, too, by golly!

What must have gone through Harvey's head
    as Joe dug in just then?
No doubt a mix of pluck and dread
    if he was like us men.
But that game Harvey on the hill
    stood like a god on Olympus
And with another thunderbolt
    could stop Milwaukee's rumpus.

Thirty-six he had retired
    impeccably and flawless:
Three up, three down times twelve it went,
    the scorebook nearly spotless.
No one had been intact this long;
    no one had ever had to.
No one had ever sung this song;
    let all men ever try to.

Oh, somewhere in this favored land
    the sun is shining bright;
Despite the hit of Adcock
    on that cool spring Tuesday night.
Haddix took his perfect loss
    with perfect class and grace.
Would his gem be half so precious
    had he won that marathon race?

Meal Ticket

With King Carl
We have choices

Remember him for his mass murder
(Ruth Gehrig and Foxx on twelve tosses)
Of the row of stars in '34?
Or for throwing the game's longest whitewash
Same year he put 46 straight goose eggs up
On the enemy's scoreboard?
Or for the no-hitter or the
Twenty glorious innings in the '33 Series or the
Pair of MVPs?

With King Carl
We have choices

Unlike those who faced him in combat
They had to try hitting
The screwball from the south side
Dipping and snapping on the black edges
Control sharp as that broken glass
From the water cooler shattered
By the freak pitch's latest victim

With King Carl
We have choices

Unlike those who considered him
For enshrinement in Cooperstown —
McGraw's left arm
Hell, the game's best in the 30's
Perhaps the higher tribute was paid
By his Giants' opponents
Who crowded their dugout steps
When Hubbell pitched
To watch
And marvel
Like fans

Carl Hubbell

49

Yogi

If this guy hadn't come along
The sport would have invented him

The mobile gnome
With a gift for one-liners
That brought down the house
And roundhouse liners
That filled up the seats
Most Octobers

Yogi was the positive end
Of the New York batteries
That powered the Ring Dynasty
His collection almost three hands full
A record pile of jewelry

He caught Page and Reynolds and Raschi and Lopat
Sain and Ford and Turley and
Don Larsen's perfecto
Later he caught Duren and Arroyo
Terry and Stottlemyre and Bouton
Countless counts and calls of strikes and balls
A million squats and blocks and foul tips
And mask adjustments to protect that face

America looking at Yogi
Saw its own reflection
Kids of immigrants could dare to hope
Dare to work their way up

Clad in tools of ignorance
Was no clown, no fool
But a sage man bearing gifts:
Pearls of laughter
Peals of wisdom
Huh?
How seriously to take all this?
Exactly.

Yogi Berra

Catching Up

I had just a few sandlot seasons
On my résumé
When Mr. Schiller down the street
An umpire at the local Little League field
Invited me to play
The catch was
I had to catch

I was a skinny kid
Wore glasses like Bill Virdon
And saw myself safer
A Pluto
In the deep orbit of
Centerfield
Not overheated Mercury
Covered with dust
And ignorant tools

Ten summers later
I donned the mask
Protector and bulky mitt
And fell in love
With the squat position
From then on
If I wasn't on the mound
I wanted to be
Sixty and a half feet away

I never did play Little League
I regret that I was such a slow learner
About backstopping
But last spring
My son's team's catcher
Had to leave the game early
And guess which assistant coach
Volunteered to fill in
A tiny gap in my life

Only two innings
And I was sore the next day
But it was worth it.

Josh

There's more about him that we don't know
Than what we know

We know he played the game hard
His black power
Generating as many stories and legends
As long balls
Hits that dared to go
Where no horsehide had gone before

His Grays and Crawfords were teams
To reckon with
'Specially when Satchel was throwing
Radio balls and B-balls
And Buck Leonard batted cleanup

If only the doors had opened sooner
Maybe we would recall Babe
As the white Josh Gibson

Smoky

The little round man
From North Carolina
Shake rattle and roll
On the bases
Could wake him up
In the middle of winter
And he'd hit a line drive
They said
Cold off the bench
His manager's southern comfort
In the heat of the pinch

In a pick-up game
You'd probably look at Burgess
And pass, choosing the tall kid
Or the one who ran fastest
Then you'd spend the rest of the day
Regretting he wasn't on your side

Something about him was familiar
He was the shape of your dad or uncle
Had the face of your neighbor
A gas station attendant
With the swing of a lumberjack

When a score of squatting seasons
Took their toll
He became a pure hitter
As naturally as always
Long before the rule
He was designated

Unamuno was right:
Comparisons are odious
But he hit ten points higher than Yogi
Nineteen over Campy, with more hits
And twenty-eight above Johnny, whom he out-tripled
Maybe what keeps him out of Cooperstown
Is that Smoky let his bat
Do all the talking

Immortal

What makes Charlie hustle after Ty
And Hank hammer at the Babe's mountains?

Why are hurlers drawn to the number 300
Batters to 3,000
Like moths to the stadium lights
On a hot August night?

Somewhere between their rookie swings and flings
Some season closer to the end of the line
The light went on and started to pull

Until then they were satisfied
To climb up the ranks of league leaders
To squeeze out the best years they could manage
Numbers were ammunition at contract times

Suddenly they stood on those stats
Layers of digits onion-thin alone
But accumulated
They support the man on tiptoes
Head in the clouds and dreaming
Of immortality
Baseball style

Now they are no longer just hitting
But climbing
Notch by notch
A strikeout closer to Gaylord or Fergy or Sandy
A double to go to catch Gehrig for fifteenth
How many DPs to turn before Maz is passed?
Now they are wondering how their plaque might go
If they make the Hall
Or if not
What might be chiseled
On their tombstone for
All time

Bang the Drum Slowly

(A Review)

Bruce Pearson is Everyfan
Wanting only to be one of the guys
In the action somehow
Whether tegwar or
The Game

Ragged
He struggles at the plate
Ought to be sent down
And forgotten

The sweet irony
Is that things turn around
By the simple revelation
Of his mortality
Something everybody already
knew
Right?

The parable succeeds
Because Everyfan really does
flourish
When included
Remembered
Treated with the respect
That their brief time in the Show
Deserves

Father

Teenage immigrant
From the land of rounders
Henry caught the New York strain
Of the national virus
Soon to be pastime

The seedling sport
Was without foliage
When this son of a
Journalist
Came along to tend
Its all–American growth

His pen swatted away
Its pesky attackers
As his prose nurtured
Like gentle sunlight
Its rooting
And its climb heavenward

Editor of guides
Chronicler of rule books
He watched and weeded
Wrote and seeded
Cultivated the shape of the game
Taught it language

Perhaps his sense of
The beauty and wonder in each contest
Was behind his skepticism of
Homers and championship games:
Let runs be earned by hits and wits
Let no inning be called meaningless

His name was penciled in
The Elysian Field lineup
But his work was all outside the lines
Recall that name
When marveling at the economy
Of the box score
The same name bronzed
In Cooperstown's Hall:
Henry Chadwick

Box Score

Chadwick's love child
Names and numbers
Abbreviations galore
Residue of action
Wrung emotionless

To properly digest
(The label might go)
Add the water of imagination
Stir well
And sip slowly
Like wake-up coffee

The stadium scoreboard
Reproduced in miniature
Tells the taller tale
But stories lurk
In every column and line

Yet for all it reveals
Of connections between
Bats and balls
More is concealed:
Skeletons have
No expression
Nor do the dry bones
Of poetry in motion

Gunner

(The Voice of the Pirates)

Bob Prince's voice
Was reflected in his sportcoats:
Colorful and loud
Mostly original
Above all comfortable

The sandpaper sound carried farther
(The wind was a factor)
Than Dick Stuart's homers
To Pirate fans in exile
From the friendly confines of Forbes
Connecting them with the battlefront

His nicknames stuck like Superglue
Making the players a little more familiar
And the game a little more fun

Sometimes he was so full of—
Baseball Stuff—
That you became so mad
You wanted to heave your scorebook
Through the radio
But you couldn't
And then he made you feel
Like you were in the upper deck
On the other end of a Stargell slam
And when he finally trotted out
"We had 'em ALLLLL the way"
You were laughing and crying
And wondering what time to tune in
Tomorrow night

Every house that KDKA reached became
A House of Thrills
Not by a gnat's eyelash either
Or the length of a green weenie
But by a country mile

We can never quite kiss goodbye
The echoes of his calls
Any more than we can forget
The way we were when we just listened
To partner-in-banter Possum
And that son of a Gunner
Who made every game a home game

Genesis

Some believe it began
When the primordial cosmic egg hatched:
Horsehide tearing loose stitch by stitch
And the S-shaped halves falling away
To reveal tablets of stone
Etched with mystic numbers
(Such as 90' and 60'6")
And commandments that permitted stealing
And great immutable words
Like "Choose sides"
And "Play ball!"

In the beginning
(Another myth has it)
Was Abner
Who separated barbaric stakes and foul terrain
From civilized bases in a fair field
Freeing men from profane sticks and wickets
With a simple sacred sphere
Wringing harmony out of chaos
At the *axis mundi* Town of Cooper

Legends ripe with morals
Outside historians' domain
Are in the end all eschatological:
Betraying our deepest longing
For green paradise to be found
Around the hallowed mound
Freed by rules and rituals
For timeless joy

Baseball Encyclopedia

Open the cornucopia
And feast:

Look up the kid from
Your high school
Your town
From that game you saw
As a kid
As a newlywed
As a dad
As gramps

Look up the season
You saw your first game
The first time you
Were one of thirty thousand

How about the year we
Won the pennant
Or the one we remember
Slightly better
When we came so close
Look it up

It tells all:
How many they hit and missed
How many lost and won and saved
Where they played
And how well
As they suitcased
From team to team

Not even Shakespeare
Could have invented
All of the glorious
Nicknames

Not even Casey
Could have dreamed
All of the stuff
You could look up here

Transformers

In the game
We strove for
The perfect play:

My pal Bill
Would crack
A towering
Fungo fly

Whose arc peaked
Exactly midway between
Him and the wall

(The wall:
Covered with ivy
Like Wrigley or Forbes
And sloping
To accommodate
Outfielders of
Any height)

There I stood
Ready to leap
Feeling the ivy
With my bare hand
Then stretching heavenward
With my glove open
To transform the
Game-winning homer
Into the final out
As the fans go wild

Opening Day

The countdown is over at last
Boswell said it best:
Time is ready to begin

The hopes and fears of winter
Start looking for foundation
In the first at-bats and pitches
That count

Take the first step
Of the thousand mile journey to October
Everything feels symbolic
Field day for the superstitious

Boxscores for breakfast tomorrow
Rotations to try and examine
Rookies to scrutinize
Favorites to root on

Radios break their silence
TV glimpses into arenas
Next best thing to being
Out with the crowd

For kids
Opening day wins
Stir visions of fall bunting
Draped around the home upper deck

For those with twenty or thirty
April launch memories
The pageantry amuses and reminds
And stirs a little bit
Of the kids inside

Name words more magical than
Play ball

First Game

Mine was at Forbes
Bucs and Cubs
Saturday matinee
General admission

Sat behind first base
Back of the Pirate dugout
But before the game
We got close enough to
Recognize
Faces from our cards

I forget who won
But I remember
Dale Long

The year before
He homered
In eight straight games
Putting Pittsburgh
On the baseball map
For a week

But now he wore visitors' gray
Traded mid-season to Chicago
Just like my parents' hero Kiner

Now he was back in the smaller town
And we still cheered him
Like family

Proving that
Once in love, always in love
Happens
Over and over

Little League

I don't know about you
But when I was a kid
We played ball
As far away from the adults
As we could get

It was OK if someone's dad
Wanted to join in and play *with* us
To make the sides even
(And to keep the arguments brief
And the fights even briefer)
Grownups made fine umps

But it was clearly our game
We called the strategy
Bunted if we wanted to
Sneak on base
Try the hidden ball trick
Or throw sidearm

Just let some adult
Try to tell us how to hold the bat!
We'd announce who we were that time up
Mantle or Mays
We'd crouch crooked like Musial
Or try to slash like Clemente
No one knew which would work best
For them
But we knew who we ought to imitate
And we had fun
Doing it

The Man

As kids we copied everything big league
Willie's basket catches
Spahnie's high-kicking delivery
Maz's twin-killing pivot at the keystone
Then there was Stan's stance

We could imitate it all right
Peek out around the corner
Coiled question mark
Ready to explode into a double
Slash the up outside pitch over third
Or off the right-center scoreboard
Yank the low inside one
Over the screen in right

Never happened
What worked so well for Musial
The durable Cardinal
Was folly for us to try
We were posing
Trying to look like the hitter
The natural Man

Good thing he never played Little League
Coaches would have straightened him out
And the rest
As they say
Would not be history

Stan Musial

Four Hundred

Shoeless Joe did it as a rookie
Burkett and Sisler did it twice
Cobb and Hornsby thrice
'Twas done lots before the century
Turned
Into the era where
.400 hitters
As Keeler might put it
Ain't

So with each passing winter
We wonder if Ted's
Summer of '41
Means the breed's extinct

Night ball
Plane trips
Big gloves
Bullpens

It's because everything's better
Or maybe because everything's worse
In the game where nothing essential
Changes

Perhaps the greatest change
Is that Cobb & Co.
Expected
To do it
While today
Nobody does
So nobody does it

Perhaps we fans
Are partly to blame
For the slump
Of tomorrow's inhabitants
Of Cooperstown
We've lowered the price
Of admission
And paid the price

Memphis Bill

Who knows what he'd have done
Had baseball been his life
And not just his livelihood?

This cream of a hitter
Rose to the top of the game
Slowly: rookie at 27
First basemen in New York
Had to be superstar material
And Bill Terry fit the bill fine

We remember him for his glove
As well as that scorching bat
That made his home park opponents
Wish they had polo horses
To chase his liners in the gaps

In that wild summer of the Bat
When practically everyone hit .300
Terry hit .4(01)—
Last in his league to ascend
That privileged peak

Who knows what he'd have done
Had he been on speaking terms
With his boss
Those two silent seasons?
Yet McGraw named Terry
To carry on the Giant fight
And add to their NL flag collection

We remember Mgr. Bill for asking
If Brooklyn was still in the league
(New York turns whispers into headlines)
And for playing in the majors as if
He was ready to be called up

Bill Terry

The Sizzler

Toss a shutout against Walter Johnson
Hit four hundred twice
Get more hits in a season
Than anyone before or since
Play your position with elegance
Regularly leading your league
In assists and DPs
Steal fifty
Do all that and more
And they might compare you to
George Sisler

His Cooperstown bat required more games
Than pitching would permit
So he made the Ruthian switch
One less southpaw in the rotation
But oh that grace in the field
And prowess in the daily lineup

George was the guy who seemed quiet
By Roaring Twenties standards
His 41 was the league's streak mark til Joe D.
Eclipsed like the .420 that he
Painted with strokes of genius
Forty-two ounce brush
On horsehide canvas
Humbly initialed
The other George H.

George Sisler

Drag Bunt

No grand slam
No long hit, really
Matches the beauty
Of this marvelous
Four-second
Feat

Timing
As usual
Is everything

To catch the pitch
With the bat
Ever so gently
Just the right spot
Just the right speed
Just right

Then to direct
The pill
Perfectly past
The hurler
Pulling in
The tall fielder
With the long mitt

And all the while
Sprinting
For all you're worth
Because a man on
Can be the break
In the dam
And the start
Of the necessary
Rally

Say Hey

Recall Willie for "The Catch"
His four-dinger day or his 660
Or for a tackle:

His Giants were battling on the road
Sunday's twin bill was crucial
Conditions ripe for basebrawl
Just a matter of time
Til the beanballs drew warnings
Baking dugouts spilled their contents
To converge in a dogfight in the dust

Willie sacked his teammate with the bat
As if to say
Hey, it's a *game*

Willie said the same thing
With every slick basket catch and
Pulled triple over third
He could excite a crowd
With a foul ball

His face lit up the field
Mays played each game
All-Star showcase
And October classics included
As if he were on the other side
Of that wall in center
Out in the streets
The biggest kid in the stickball game
The one who made the game fun
Joy to the world

Willie Mays

A Play in the Life

Say Willie Mays
And where does your imagination run?
You know where:
To the Polo Grounds
October of '54
Vic Wertz up for the Tribe
Score tied
Late innings
Game One of the Series

Crack

And the Say Hey Kid is off
Back to the diamond
We see the white blur descend
Behind number twenty-four
Over the moving shoulders
Into the precious leather glove
Then it's shot back
Like a slapped ping-pong ball
Out of Willie's hatless whirl

The film we've seen over and over
Usually includes a cut to the crowd
Holding their heads in awe and relief
Witnesses to the crime
To which they'll testify
With pleasure and pride
All of their tomorrows

Radio Nights

It's nightfall
And the sky is coming alive
With the unmistakable sounds
Of baseball

Fish in a zone
For the familiar voices of
The hometown
Its local commercials
Comforting accent
And above all its wonderful bias
In the play by play
Give it away

Or trawl across the numbers
And see what you can pull in:
Boston flounders teasing New Englanders
Mixed with Baltimore fare
Between the Pennsylvanians' perches
West of these catches
Sift for the Cardinals in there
Chisox & Reds at the south of the dial
Jays up north
Know where they lurk
In the swirling currents of darkness

Rookies at the craft
Don't take long to learn how to
Focus on the crowds out there
Their buzz so distinct from static
Their roars often enough
To hint at scores
Before the update
And sign-off

The Crab

Trojan at the Cub keystone
Middleman in the Adams poem as
Chance would have it
No reason to
Tinker with the lineup
Evers was the plotting manager's
Choice to lead the way to
October's game

Johnny was on the spot in '08
When Merkle made his infamous
Giant boner—
"Touch all the bases"
Credit Evers with an assist
On the cliché

Give him another A
For the Miracle in Boston
Pulled with the Rabbit
Out of the basement hat

In shallow or deep
Hard-shelled combatant
Inventor of strategy
As rough on those in blue
As on the invaders of his sack
Eye on the horsehide
As well as the cleat
Thinker Evers
Really left little to
Chance

Johnny Evers

73

Mechanical Man

His lack of color
Was legendary
All he did was
Hit throw and field
With the All-Star efficiency
Of a machine

Charlie Gehringer was a
Vacuum at the keystone
Turn him on and he
Keeps his turf clean
With monotonous consistency
Preventing build-up on the basepaths
Sweeping away enemy rallies
Making it look effortless

Charlie Gehringer was a
Robobatter at the plate
Turn him on and he
Sorts out the pitches
Worth his swings
Automatically
Racks up two hundred safeties a season
Drives in a hundred or so
And all with such showmanship
That come time to vote for MVP
You scratch your head for his name
This Tiger roared
With his leather and wood

Hands

Much is made
Of the hands
Of the artist
The surgeon
The carpenter

I marvel at the hands
Of the infielder
Whose magic moves
Convert hits
Into double plays

Precision
Grace
Timing
Even artistry

Bless the wizard
Whose grasp is sure
Whose toss is true
And strong enough
To nip the runner
And the rally

Stolen Base

Baseball memories are sticky:
My earliest has me on the sidelines
While Mom and Mick and Sue
Are in the game
(While Dad plays tennis nearby)
At North Park

I must have tired
Of the hitting and running
When I picked up third base
And wandered off to read it

Mom was the victim tagged out
Gotcha!
No FAIR!
Who's got third?

Forty years later
We still laugh about it
And argue whether I took
A Golden Book or comic

Cool Papa

Legend has him racing his own hits
To second base
Faster than the speed of light
Going out in the bedroom
Scoring from first
On bunts
Stealing two bases
On a pitchout
A sprinter whose feats
Inspired mythic tales
And grew in the telling

Anchor man Jackie
And Monte
And all to whom Bell passed
The black baton
Finished the relay

Fitting that the man who was
A blur on the basepaths
Should become a symbol for
A page in the sport's history
Blurred itself by tears and wonderings
Of what might have been

Look up speed in the baseball dictionary:
Cool Papa Bell has already been there
And is sliding past your finger
Around your tag
Can't touch him
To score

His seasons were filled with movement
Dusty bus trips between towns
Made longer by the searches
For places where blacks were welcome
To eat or sleep or be
Made longer by the searches
For clean socks and sweatshirts
To wear in the third game of the day
Made longer by the searches
For the day when all their deeds afield
Might be written down
In scorebooks and newspapers
Might be written in black and white
Might be dignified by the recognition
They happened

76

Black Mike

Once upon a time
Catchers
Were armored backstops
Not expected to hit and run
And push their teams to win
With the fury of a general
In love with trench warfare

Mickey Cochrane
Raged to pennants
With MVP fire in his eyes
The A's of Connie Mack
And then his own Tigers

The teams caught *him*

What ended that day in May
When Mickey's skull was suddenly split
By the high inside heater?
The summers of .300 swings
In combat focused squarely on victory
His squatting battle cries silenced
Energy spent at last
His mark on the game
Etched indelibly

Mickey Cochrane

Maz

Coal miner's son
Wizard
Of his seasons
Object of awe
From fellow All-Stars
His small tattered glove
Ripened into gold

His stats dazzle
Far less
Than his craft
Yet they glow
Mightily

Pirate pitchers
In trouble
And fans alike
Prayed aloud
For deliverance
From a rally:
Hit it to Maz

Master of the
Six-four-three cascade
Artist of the forces:
Four-six and four-three
Balladeer of the saving
Two!
Maker of mystic DPs
Fabled POs and A's—
The uncommon E's
Only served as reminders
That he was of this world
After all

Might as well
Recall Ruth
Strictly for his
Fielding
As believe Bill Mazeroski
Can be summed
In that infamous
Clout

The Fan

Who sank the Yanks?
Was it Maz
Or did he merely
Swing the bat
At the opportune time?
Study all the film
As if you were looking
For assassins
Hiding in the corner
Of a frame
Featuring a Dallas motorcade
What do you see?
Terry hurling the 1–0 fastball
The now-famous Pirate batter swinging
The collision in that
Twilight strike zone
Over the plate
Now you see Berra cursing
The ivied wall that
Prevents the catch

But wait!
Back up a few frames
THERE
There she is:
The lady in that weird hat
Wearing the same kind of glasses
As my mother
SHE'S DOING IT!
Her hands are aloft
Fingers trembling
Palms tilting slightly heavenward
As she follows the ball's airy path
She's holding her breath
LOOK AT HER EYES!
Don't tell me she's not
Guiding the object in flight
Over Yogi
Over the brick barricade
To somewhere over the rainbow

Maz is pounded as he soars home
As if he did it himself
But throughout the stadium
And the city
The pounding goes on
Of his
Accomplices

Nap

Never played in a Series
Denied the national light of October
That might have linked his name
With some great catch or smash
Made it household

What survives of his time in the game
Besides his numbers
Is that marvelous name

Whole afternoons can be spent
Arguing how to pronounce it
Not Napoleon of course
But the other part

And Lajoie turns up all over:
Lists of your average kings
Keystone wizards
Dynamic doublers
The 3M Club
The Hall

Sooner or later
You had to pitch to him
Sooner or later
We need to learn how
To say his name right
If we want to talk baseball

Nap Lajoie

Unassisted Triple Play

Only happened once so far
In the Series

Bill Wambsganss
(Was his family really so poor
They couldn't afford to buy a vowel?)
Was in precisely the right place
For stepping out of time
Into baseball eternity

From his position at second
Wamby took a running leap
And snagged fame
With an easy trot to the sack
And a gentle tap on the shoulder
Of the runner from first

Who can say which snakebite
Stunned the Brooklynites more
In that pivotal fifth game:
The first Series slam in the first
Or Wamby's gem in the fifth?

Argue on
Whether the leather
Is mightier than the wood

Just remember
To spell the name right

Rajah

He took his stand
As distant from the pitcher
As he could possibly be
Without being outside
The white rectangle
Waited
Focused
With eyes he reserved
(No moving picture shows—
Or reading)
Saved for that horsehide
Bound to be ambushed
On its trip to the mitt
Doomed to be converted into
Another counter in the
H column to the right of
Hornsby's name in
Tomorrow's box score

In the family album
Rogers' place is as secure
As his niche in Cooperstown
As certain as his name
In any hot stove debate
About the greatest hitter
Ever

But somehow we are quick to turn
    the page
Move on to faces less stern
Uncles far less successful
Or who drank too much
They left behind kind memories

Hornsby stares at us
From his swirling world of
Unthinkable sums of money
Betting on the horses
Getting on the nerves
Of everyone in his path
As if he is still taking a stand
As distant from us
As he can possibly be
Without being outside
This imperfect clan

Rogers Hornsby

Squeeze

Suddenly
It's do or die
The moment of truth
And consequence

Your teammate
Is barreling home
With all he's got
And more:
If he scores
Your team wins
And you're the hero

All that needs to be done
Is to stop the
White blur
Before it splats
Into the mitt
Behind you

If you miss
Your teammate's out
Number three
And you
A step closer
To being sent back
To where you were
Last season
When you played
Eighty games
In between
Bus rides

Pie

Rhymes with eye
As in batting
Look up contact hitter
And Traynor will be there
Sure as he was there
Turning the smash over the bag
From a double to a five-three
With a hunk of leather
That deserved no assist on the play

In a city with its own way of talking
Pie never lost his
Over seventeen loyal seasons
Pittsburgh adopted him
Like a favorite son

He was no specialist
So his batsmanship
Baserunning and feats afield
Guarding the hot corner
All glow equally
From our distance

The Game's greatest third baseman?
Calling Pie the best would not
Swell his head then
Nor add to his stature now
He carved out his Cooperstown niche
Like a Robert Frost spinning a poem
With quiet dignity
Hard work
Grace
Leaving behind a sport
That now spoke
With a little of his accent

Hot Corner

(*In Memory of Don Hoak, 3B*)

Not for the timid
Third base needs
Tigers

Reflexes of a cat
Ready and able to pounce
On the topped bleeder
Dive to either side
For the shot
Off the pitcher's mistake
Leap and knock down
The would-be double
Use your chest
Like a shield
Never give up
Pick it up bare-handed
Just got 'em

This sack
Is where things converge
Spikes-high enemies
Looking for a springboard
Ninety feet from victory
Fielders' tosses in the dust
Aiming to sever
The rally
The eyes of umps and cameras
Wait to see the impacts
As you straddle
Block
Brace

Let pilots cruise the warning track
And sailors pitch
Third is for Marines

Arky

Wagner's protégé
And heir to his slice of the turf
Vaughan could do it all
But quietly

Arky's bat
Rippled with triples
And painted .300 seasons
With constancy and verve
His Mona Lisa 1935
Still shimmers and dazzles

Arkansas polished gem
That displayed its facets best
On the All-Star diamonds
Hard substance
On collision course
With the Lip of Brooklyn

Had the patience for ball fours
And the eye to spoil fouls
Would rather retire at 31
Support the war on his farm
Than give in to Durocher
Stayed offstage for over three
Prime seasons
For his own unstated
Prime reasons

In uniform
We only saw a man at work
Out of it
We saw a man who wanted to decide
Himself
Whom to call Boss
That's important to some folks

Trades

They happen
Not as often as in
Antediluvian (Curt, that is) days
Before pawns could speak
Before they could plod to the last rank
And become royalty

But they still happen
Still compete with blizzards for headlines
Still sadden, delight, puzzle and promise
Cause fans to ponder the numbers
Compare the new apples and the old oranges
With suspicion and hope

No trade is guaranteed
The teeth of the steed
Tell not his speed
Nor the odds of his post-stumble need
To be shot

Hall of Famers have been traded
(Or—pardon the word—sold)
Before, during or after their primes
Goes to show
You never know
What you've let go
In the Player to be Named

And how would you like it
If they named you
Later?

Astroturf

The first time I saw it
It so reminded me of our old basement pool table
Felt stretched green and tight over immovable slabs
That I wondered why the horsehides didn't click
Like dropped cue balls
Instead of bouncing like rubber

Having played some on uneven sandlot infields
I could *appreciate* the plastic rugs
But never really felt comfortable with them

Not because of all the reasons I heard
That players baked on it during shorter careers
That it changed the defense
Outfield and in
Or that horses wouldn't eat it

No, it was simply that
I had never played on the stuff
And so a link was missing
Between all of *my* games
And all of
Theirs

Bleachers

Barzun was right:
Men are happy here

Fans getting tans
Exposed to the elements

Waiting patiently
On cloudy days
For drops of rain
Or pitchers' mistakes

Grandstand

The roof giveth
And the roof taketh away

Shelter from
Foul balls
And foul weather

Protector of
Souvenir scorecards

Haven of vendors
And those who
In real life
Long
To move up a notch
From General Admission

Georgia Peach

Like all kids
I was fascinated by dinosaurs:
No family visit to the museum
Was without its long pause
In their Hall
Where the fiercest of all
Tyrannosaurus Rex
Towering over cowering crowds
Commanding fear and respect
Ruled

Like all kids
I was impressed by big numbers
And another Ty's stats towered
As tall over the sport
As that museum reptile's skeleton over me
Over all but the Babe

Later I learned
Ruth had won the hearts of all America
While Cobb won hardly a friend
As if his file-sharpened spikes
Had gashed the ankles of the nation
Who thought they were in it for fun

They said he played like a man possessed
And maybe this Georgian was
Haunted by his father's ghost
To excel at any cost
And it cost him dearly

I imagine the last tyrannosaurus
Facing extinction
Got little sympathy
From those once terrorized
Their scars reminders
That some breeds
Need to rule
Their own cruel league
At any cost

Ty Cobb

90

Scars and Spikes

There sat Ty
Not in the dugout's shadows
But out in the sunlight
Out on the top step
Sending his message
Filing his spikes
Blood in his mind's eye

How many throws went awry
During infield practice
As the basemen found themselves
Unable to keep from peeking
Out of the corners
At the ritual

Cobb did it all right
The stories are not myths
Clues to the man's soul
Fables embellished
To send shudders
Down young spines
And widen the eyes of those
Who see the game
As sport
And not war

The tales were first told
You see
By men with scars

Pete Rose

To be or not to be
Admitted to the Hall:
That's the hot stove question
Fueling our coming to grips
With what the Hall is
And is not

It is not a pantheon
And though we pilgrimage there
We dare not worship

The Hall is still but a place
That recalls and honors great deeds
And their doers
And while we remember
Admire with awe
And gain inspiration
We must concede
That those honored
Simply played exceedingly well
An all too human game

Let he who is without
Cast the first
Ballot without
The old Red Rose:
So ruled the slain umpire

In the interim or forever
Fate has chosen the
Most fitting punishment
For this hitter:
Condemned to the on-deck circle
Rolling like Sisyphus
His stone of lost innocence
Up the Cooperstown slope
Only to see it heaved back down
By cowardly gods
Knowing not themselves
Nor what they defend

The Hall

(Memories of First Visit, 1965)

Ty Cobb's
Well-worn sliding pads
Got my attention

Along with gloves
Flat as pancakes
Balls ringed
With proud autographs
Bats retired
To hang forever silent
Having boomed
Something famous

A dream attic filled
With once-upon-a-time
Surrounding a chapel:
Through its bronze windows
Gaze its gods

If Yankee Stadium
Is the House that Ruth Built
Then in Cooperstown
Is the one
He furnished

The Kid

Final day of the season
The choice is to sit it out
And go down in history with the handful
Of .400 hitters
Or play the doubleheader

The numbers that spell Ted best
May be that six-for-eight
Knocked out while on the ledge
Baseball immortality on the line
Crux of a legend
Williams accepted the dare

Too much for a single nickname
Splinter for opposing arms
Splendid for the Fenway swarms
Seemed a veteran of foreign war
Even before Korea
Triple-Crown Thumper
Who had to have the
Last turn at bat
In Teddy's Ballgame

Ted Williams

The Game in Between

Over a century ago
The debate started:
Is baseball a brain game
A chess match of strategy
Cunning
Imagination —
A duel between
Confidences?

Or is it all brawn
Strength vs. strength
A slugfest contest
Where power pitching
And contact hitting
Eclipse the value of
The manager's ideas?

Argue not
Either/Or:
Baseball is the rare event
Played out between spirit and matter
Between mind and muscle —
Its arena is the very synapse
Between the axons and dendrites
Of our humanness

So it is a Game
For all seasons
Subjective and objective
For gray matter
For green grass
And the rainbow of reality
In between

Home Run

Good thing J. Franklin
Played ball back then
Or he'd wear the tag
Dinger or Tater
Or Gopher!

This fabulous Baker boy
Could slug the dead ball all right
Though his summer peak was
The original Baker's Dozen
His decisive October pair
Against McGraw's M-Boys
Earned him the nickname:
Right place and time
For the dubbing

Connie Mack's
Hot corner man
In the $100,000 Infield
(Four stars for
Pinch-hitter's wages —
Those were the days)
The speedster with sock
Wielded a three-and-a-quarter pounder
Sturdy ungiving spar
Not unlike the wagon tongues on
His quiet Maryland farm

Frank summered there twice
In his playing days:
Casualty in the Federal League War
And then to be with his dying wife
Home Run Baker knew when
To step back from the game
And choose the heavier
Burdens

Frank Baker

The Bat

Its shape
Is found nowhere
In nature

Yet it feels natural
To grip
To squeeze with both palms
The space above its knob
To let it sway
Like a branch
The perfect extension
Thirty-something inches
Of the arms
To cradle
And inspect
For sweet spots

Thirty-two ounces
Two pounds
To pound

White ash
Plucked from Pennsylvania
To become not just
A Louisville Slugger
But a craftsman's tool
In pursuit of fun
Or glory

Hammerin' Hank

Before Jackie broke the color line
Hank hammered at similar stuff
Learning when to take
And when to swing
On and off the diamond

Greenberg's might
Produced a storm of Tiger runs
Near-record summers of
Round-trippers and ribbies

His career almost suggests
An answer to
"How do you get to Cooperstown?" —
"Practice, practice, practice!"

When the Tigers needed first base
For Rudy York
Hank could relate to that
Needing first base
Was why he chose Detroit
Over the Stadium
Where Gehrig ruled

This team player
Could not ride the bench
In the battle after Pearl Harbor
His Air Corps heroics
Grandly recalled after the struggle
When his slam in the final '45 game
Took his team into the Series

Greenberg was a giant
An awkward kid from the Bronx
Who grew into a polished pro
A Goliath with the soul of David

The Gray Eagle

Tris perched in shallow center
Like a bird of prey
Taking off on wings for any fly
Soaring with his back to the infield
With uncanny rehearsed instinct
Ballhawk threw out runners
With deadly accuracy
And in record numbers
Texan in his own league
Speaker
COVERED
Centerfield

Sharp eye at the plate
Same speed that
Ran down would-be hits
Stretched plenty of singles
Into two-baggers
Tris might have been tagged
Baseball's Mister Double

If Adams had been stung
By the Boston outfield trio's arms
Instead of the Cubbie DP combo
Tris might have wound up
Immortalized in verse between
Hooper and Lewis

But Tris Speaker
Was not about might-have-beens
His deeds at bat and afield
Over twenty-two summers
Played fierce and proud
As an eagle

Tris Speaker

Master Melvin

It must have been
Love at first sight:
The dead-pull hitting kid
Just over his first glimpse of New York
Standing at the plate and gazing
With wonder and delight
To where the Polo Grounds' right field ended
Less than a hundred yards away
There lay what for two decades
Would be known as Ottville

Time was on his side
No need to rush things
The teen had time to go to school
On the bench beside Mr. McGraw
Time to ease into the lineup
To start making history

The energy he saved up
Signing autographs —
Six letters and "Next, please" —
Poured into his game:

Eccentric but disciplined
High-kicking right leg
Pounding down as the pitch is studied
Arcing bat springing around
For the launch;
Marvelous snares and snags
When he roamed far from McGraw's dugout
Yet within armshot of the base ahead
Of the larcenous runners
Arrested by his gun

Mel Ott was a sixty-nine inch tall
Hundred and seventy pound Giant
Pitchers would just as soon walk him
Rather than face his game-breaking
Mel Ott Unmistakable presence

Within Two and Without Two

Within two outs of victory
The dam burst
The last-ditch enemy rally
Threatened to eclipse
The six-run lead built up
So carefully
Run by precious run
Over the first eight innings

Now with five in and
The sacks full of trouble
We were still within two

And the DP was do-able
This batter was no speed merchant
And sure enough he topped one
Up the middle
The play at the keystone
Went smoothly
As the runner hurled his torso
In vain
Under the leaping middleman
And the race was on

Without two
The game would be tied
The inning alive
And the on deck white
Circled their hottest bat
Aching for a headline

White spurted from first base
As the long mitt's leather clapped
And we all had to check
The black-sleeved right arm
Of the kneeling squinting ump
To see we had come up
Without two

Roberto

No scorecard necessary
To tell who Number 21 was:

Clemente threw lasers at the bases
Terrorizing enemy baserunners
Or preventing them
With lazy basket-catches
Or streaking stabs
With leaps at the wall
Or dives along the foul line
Habitually converting doubles
To nines in the scorebook
Or reducing them to singles
He was a master of the carom

Roberto ran as no other
Slashing away at the wind
That dared hold him back
From his journey home
Leaving behind his helmet
And caution
Arriba!

Of course his hits
Would total a perfect
Three thousand
Before he was suddenly lost
Post-season:
The time for character
Always his brightest time

Responding to Nicaraguans
In the wake of an earthquake
Clemente stepped onto the plane
From the on-deck circle
Of a life of unorthodox intensity

Roberto played proud
And made proud
His land and race
And the city
So far from where
In the dark of
New Year's Eve
The star fell

Roberto Clemente

Mine

I got it, I yelled
Waving my glove high
Over my head
And back-pedaling
Into the outfield

Mine, the ominous voice
From left
Rumbled over my right shoulder
Over his incoming footfalls

All mine, the high-pitched centerfielder
Screamed
Waving us both away
As we all converged
On the plummeting white blur
At Ground Zero

Mine
We harmonized
In the last second before—
The Hit—
Was ruled a triple

Got It

My dad and I
Had front-row field box seats
For a Sunday game against Philly
At old Forbes Field
And arrived early to watch BP
Up close

A super-scuffed practice ball
Rolled our way and stopped
An empty box away

Too easy
But I had my souvenir
Signed by the NL President
Hassle-free

The next day
It would look like a line drive
In the story I'd tell my friends
Before we put the ball
Back in play

Baseball Beatitudes

Happy the pitcher ahead in the count
    For he shall inherit more outs
    Than hits against.

Happy the defense that retires the leadoff man
    For they shall inherit a crucial edge.

Happy the offense that sacrifices for a run
    For they shall inherit more wins.

Happy are they who lose the game
    But win the series;

Happy are they who lose the series
    But win the week;

And happy are they who lose the week
    But win the month:
    For months outweigh weeks
    And weeks, series
    And series, games.

Happy the teams who lose the sprints
    But win the marathon:
    For they shall inherit the Playoffs.

And happy are they who play in October
    For they shall inherit
    The best memories of all.

Low and Away

When Alexander joined in
The civil war
Between pitcher and hitter
That broke out loud when
He was growing up
Pete was Ulysses—
S. Grant, that is
Battling on several fronts
The batters were easier to master
Than the alcohol and
The Prohibitionist managements

Pete's work on the diamond
Spoke louder than he—
His solitariness
An asset on the mound
When it was one on one
When a strike or shutout was needed
Pete delivered

In all the seasons between
His brilliant break-in rookie
And his inglorious clinging struggle
At the end
The war raged on
All fronts

Epilepsy confused with intemperance
Pete half-listened to or half-heard
Those outside the lines
Where he battled

Looking back we see double:
Always that image
Of the single Series save
The four clutch pitches to Lazzeri
Superimposed over two decades of deeds
Not likely to be seen again
Achieved one day at a time
The innings when Pete
Was in control

Grover Cleveland Alexander

Addie

His sudden death
Just after Opening Day 1911
When hearts were filled with sheer hope
Jolted the sport

Addie Joss after all
Had a reputation
For finishing what he started
Cleveland's consummate starter
Nine times out of ten
When the day's battlesmoke cleared
Was still there

Addie Joss after all
Was a professional
It was his job to entertain
Those who worked in dingy factories
Or on Great Lakes barges
He took his vocation as seriously
As they
So how could he not
Report to work this season?

Addie Joss after all
Was mortal
Despite his superhuman ERA
Transcendent collection
Of shutouts, no-hitters, and
Less quantifiable gems
And above all the respect
Earned from his peers

Perhaps if he'd have played longer
Eighteen or twenty summers
Instead of nine
Perhaps he'd have made more enemies
Familiarity with Addie Joss
Bred no contempt
His passing on early
Was celebrated by his leaguemates
With an impromptu All-Star game
Proceeds to his widow
The perfect wake
Weep for joy

Addie Joss

106

Matty

Matty made his opponents talk to themselves:
"What's a college boy doin' in the game
Playin' with a bunch a redneck ruffians
Who smoke 'n' drink 'n' raise hell off the field
Sunday too when
McGraw's right-hand man won't even pitch?
Pert' soon the ladies will want t' come 'n' watch
Athletes don't write no books neither
Stick wit' the checkers and bridge, Bible-toter!

"Shoot the Giant don't walk nobody
Ain't no way t' touch them damn fadeaways
Ninth inning alrea —
Shut out agai —"

Matty brought to the marriage
Just what the spouse needed
Respectability
Gave his game something to shoot for
Then and tomorrow

Take away all the glittering digits
Even the Series of zeroes
They are but shadows
Of his thoughtful artistry
Mathewson stands tall without them
In control
Spell class act
Christy

Christy Mathewson

107

Pepper

Memorize his face during BP
Once the game is on
His uniform will be no help
In identifying this smiling fellow:
The top will be the shade of the infield dirt
Even in front
From thieving belly-flops
The legs dusty and green
Stained from sliding shoelace grabs
Of would-be Texas-leaguers

Memorize his name, too
Because you won't find it
In the scorecard
Or tomorrow's box score:
John Leonard Roosevelt
Salt of the Gashouse Gang
Martin was pure Pepper

Charlie Hustle of his day
Pepper spiced up the show
For his Cardinal teammates
Between and outside the lines
"Wild Hoss of the Osage"
Left Frisch holding the reins

The stats he bequeathed
Seem too ordinary to be his
All too bland—save one:
No one else so far
Who has visited the Series
Has risen to that challenge
Quite so smartly:
His dozen hits sunk the A's in '31—
One less safety in '34
Pepper: .418 for two Octobers
Seasoning of the winning recipes

A Little Help from My Pen

He was cursed with a seven-inning arm
But blessed with the best
Lefty-righty closers
In either league

When he signs the contract next year
Ought to have them there
To do the last name

He collects the wins all right
But there was a day
When if you couldn't finish
You were done

Where have all the iron men gone?
Specialized away like the dinosaurs
Leaving behind the glorious fossils
Of those uncanny box scores
And tales worth telling
To the grandchildren

Homers RBIs and Diamonds

Picture yourself on the bench in the minors
With bus rides forever and nothing to do
Till somebody calls you to head for the airport
And see if you can hit in the Show

Homers RBIs and diamonds
Strung together like Tinker Evers & Chance
The dingers add zeroes to your paychecks
And suddenly you can afford
Anything

You're twenty-four
At the top
And dreaming of Cooperstown
And you'll get there soon enough
If only you can turn off
Those kaleidoscope eyes

She's Coming Home

Wednesday evening at five PM
While her friends watch TV
Or play softball on the other field
She's got her pony tail tucked
Under a batting helmet

When she's in the field at third
They try to bunt their way on
Until they see she can throw
Was that sidearm?
Then they try to smack it past her
Until they see
She dives in the dirt
Better than their big guy

When she swings the bat
They relax in the field
Until her line drives
Over first
Over third
Then up the middle
Make them ask
Where she learned
To hit like *that*

When she tags at third in the last inning
Waiting for the pop to right-center to fall
They know she'll go
She's been going all game

The pitcher's heart sinks
Because he knows the teammate circling the ball
Will catch it all right
But his arm is weak and wild
The catcher will brace for a collision
But there will be no stopping
The winning run

She's coming home

Little League Mom

She's there in the bleachers
'Cause he's there on the field
Her firstborn son
In his firstworn uniform
Wearing a number that's close to his age
And the name of a grocery close to home
Gray pants grass-stained green
And a dirt & red jersey
That's become a daily visitor
To the laundry room

She's terrified by the speed
Of the ball
That he has to face
Despite the helmet
With the face guard and
Where's that chest protector?
He's terrified of fanning
And gladly accepts the bruises
That come with being plunked

She cheers his swings and misses
His hits and catches
And between them all finds relief
Chatting with friends
Helping out in the concession stand
Enduring till the final out
And the final game
Of this first real springtime

She's there 'cause he's there
And they both know it somehow matters
More than either can say

The Duke

Edwin D. never wouldda made it
Hadda be the Duke of Flatbush
To rule Ebbets

Old smoothie in center
Glided into the ivy and the wood
Brooklyn's All-Star answer
To his ballad companions
Willie and the Mick

Peaked in October
Sure as the leaves outside
But he was a slugger
For all seasons

Duke was delivering
The last of his superb seasons
When I caught up with him
In my rookie year at Forbes
When he smacked one o'er the screen
The nearby barricade in right
Was he already looking ahead
To long lesser seasons in Los Angeles
Or was he already full of nostalgia
For the short porch at home?
His grin as his toe stabbed the plate
Spoke a little of both

Was this man-child of summer
Who threw 300-foot strikes
Ever at home
East coast or west
Or was he all the time waiting
With every slashing swing
And scurrying snatch
For his berth in Cooperstown?

Duke Snider

Rundown

The game began
With fielders
At first and second bases
And the runner
In between

The player
Holding the ball
Gave the signal
To start

It helped
To imagine
You were Willie Mays
If you were in the middle

Arms straight out
Like a tightrope walker
For balance
Fingers twitching
Feet shuffling in the dust
Juking
Juking
Juking
Faking the break
To first
Then taking off
With everything
To hook-slide
Around the tag
And win

Hammer

Hank assaulted the game's most famous number
The Babe's mystic 714
No one was supposed to be able
To scale that Everest
Surely the air was too thin
The terrain too tricky
And the pressure
Crushing

But 714 was there
The climb had to be made

Destined by his Aa to rank first
Hank seemed to grow stronger each summer
While others slowed and wound down
He climbed on

Destined by his color to rank second
Hank seemed more outspoken each season
While others quietly accepted the rules
He climbed on

Passing all the sacred numbers
Despite the heat of Georgia
Beyond the resting place of Cooperstown
Aaron climbs on yet:
Raising up the Game
With his innings left

Henry Aaron

Frankly Speaking

What makes hot dogs
Taste better
At the ball park
Than anywhere else?

Can't be the brand
Or the roll
Or the mustard

I think it's
The process
Of spotting
The vendor
Ordering over
The noise of
The fans
Passing your bucks
To the right
And watching
The dog
Move from hand to hand
To the left

Then looking up
And rejoining the
Miracle play
In progress
Becoming again an active
Part of the hopefuls
Eating quickly
So you can keep score again
And clap along
With the kids over there
Chanting
WE WANNA *HIT*!

Home & Away

It's a game we play
In the land where you gotta have heart
Where diamonds are loose in the sky
Shining for the benefit of night games
That if won
Make for good mornings

I manage an out-of-gashouse gang
We're within two games of the cellar
And without two necessary
Pennant ingredients:
We've got to get hitting better
And to fix a hole in the rotation
Stop the traffic to the early showers
With a little help from the pen

Thank God for my lovely wife Rita
She's at home for me
Whether we've had the best
Day in the life of the franchise
Or when I'm 64–98
Come October

She lives outside my land
Out where diamonds are hard and small
And shine for the benefit of night games
That make for good mornings

I wear the gray there
She wears it here
Home and away
Home and away

Country

Enos made that Chicago word
Slaughter
Congenial to St. Louis
Easy to spot on the field
The man in motion
Hustling extra bases
Spraying clutch hits
Corner to corner

In the clan's album
Enos is the relative
We are tempted to remember
By a single photograph
One war over
Another to wage
His furious race home
Series-winning run strapped
On his bent back
Warrior back where he belonged
Tasting victory
In the charge

Gingerly we tuck behind that picture
Smaller ones
His Southern discomfort
With the family's first
Interracial marriage:
Failed strike
Successful spike—
Not to hide them
But to secure them better
Lest we forget

Not just some
But all of the pictures
Of Enos' life
Suggest the nickname
Country

Enos Slaughter

Mood Swings

He greets the day after
His team loses a toughie
Like it was drizzling outside
And all day he walks under
A sky scuffed gray

Following a victory
He springs out to
Read all about it
Bacon and box scores
Standings and eggs
For breakfast
And sunny overhead
At least till game time

Slumps wash out whole weekends
Cancel events
Like February blizzards
Make travel uncertain
Take the icing off the
Cakes celebrating triumphs
At home or work

But strings of wins
Light up his days
With honeymoon bliss
Their ecstasies eclipsing
Any power failures on the job
Communications breakdowns
Or bad luck elsewhere
The sun always shines
Somewhere
When Casey is on a roll

Talking Baseball

Bring your cap and cushion and thermos
Jacket for the cool spring evenings
Most of all, bring the wide-eyed kids
Wearing gloves for the fouls our way

Teach 'em to enjoy batting practice
The pregame rituals in the smell of grass
Let them snag autographs down by the dugouts
Before the anthem
Even the batboy might be Cooperstown-bound!

Teach 'em how to keep score
How to appreciate the fine art
Of the pickoff throw
The squeeze bunt
Or the block of the wild pitch
That saved a base
And maybe the game

Teach 'em how to care
To hoot and holler and whoop
For the sparklers
That rate little stars
Beside the numbers you jot down
After each play.
How to boo the calls that go against
How to win with grace
And lose with dignity.

How to root
And put down roots
That might grab and hold
Forever
Bloom into a place to go
Where you're a kid
No matter how old

Walk away now
Slowly in the stadium's glow
Talking about the game you saw
Talking baseball

The Dark Side of the Calendar

Between the last
October shout
And the first
Anthem of April
Lies the deep valley
Of hot stove time

Its sounds are ugly:
Obscene clamoring
Over agents
Who are anything but
Free

Its awards are dim:
Honors won
Outside of time
Inside the season

Its activity is muted:
Trading of
Analyses for forecasts
Pitchers for hitters
And cards (in former days)
Just for fun

Its fruits are unripened:
Florida grapefruit leagues and oranges
Palm balls and trees
Farm phenoms dueling
Yesterspring's aces
For the limited lines
In the boxes of summer

Discontented winters
Melt away too too slowly

The only real question
Is why nature
Wasted hibernation
On redpolls and hamsters